Falling Into the Diaspora

poems by

MaryAnn L. Miller

Finishing Line Press
Georgetown, Kentucky

Falling Into the Diaspora

Copyright © 2023 by MaryAnn L. Miller
ISBN 979-8-88838-213-4 First Edition
All rights reserved under International and Pan-American Copyright Conventions. No part of this book may be reproduced in any manner whatsoever without written permission from the publisher, except in the case of brief quotations embodied in critical articles and reviews.

ACKNOWLEDGMENTS

Special thanks are owed to the writers who were readers and editors:

J. C. Todd, Anne Kaier, Vasiliki Katsarou and Liz Abrams-Morley. I cannot write without their steadfast support, deep skills, wisdom and good company.

Publisher: Leah Huete de Maines
Editor: Christen Kincaid
Cover Art: Will Hubscher of Easton, PA.
Author Photo: MaryAnn L. Miller
Cover Design: Elizabeth Maines McCleavy

Order online: www.finishinglinepress.com
also available on amazon.com

Author inquiries and mail orders:
Finishing Line Press
P. O. Box 1626
Georgetown, Kentucky 40324
U. S. A.

Table of Contents

Forza: A Tale of Two Mafaldas 1
Mafalda's Daughter Opens Her Notebook 2
Thunderstorms 3
Western Pennsylvania Fig 4
Queen Elena Has a Baby Girl (Again) 5
Mafaldine or Little Queens 6
Turandot Villanelle 7
Canaletto Validates My Grandmother 8
Mafalda at Twelve 9
Mafalda of Savoy at Twelve 10

Mafalda Curzi's Autograph Book 1 11

Miss Reed, Butler High School 13
A Dream of Becoming a Teacher 14
Mafalda's First Job 15
An Unexpected Dream 16
Princess Mafalda Considers a Future Husband 17
Waltzing Mafalda 18
The Wedding of Princess Mafalda 19
My Mother's Wedding 20
Mafalda's Mother-in-Law 22
The Midwife's Tambourine 24
Pasquale Finds His Wealth 25
Nonna Doula 26
From the South American Diaspora 27
Princess Mafalda Meets Her In-laws 28
Philip & Mafalda After Dinner with Hitler 29
Her Luigi 30
Enlisted 31
Little Room off the Kitchen 32
A Broken Sonnet for Growing Up 33
A Loss of Land 34

Mafalda Curzi's Autograph Book 2 35

The Work of Conception 37
Happy Times 38
Princess Mafalda's Children 39
The Princess is Almost... 40
She Recovered 41
Transported 42
Frau von Weber 43
Remembrances… 45
L'Ultima Pagina.. 47
Caption on a Map of Buchenwald.. 48
Francobollo, a Postage Stamp 1997.. 49
The Princess Stars in a Pulp Fiction…................................... 50
In Herr Doktor Schiedlausky's Words 51

Mafalda Curzi's Autograph Book 3 53

A Fall on the Stairs 55
How My Father Taught Me My Power.................................. 56
Resumption of a Dream.. 57
Something Grew.. 58
Minnesang for Both of Them... 60
Natura Morta 61
After Time & Space 62
The sedative cycle of the days… 63
I don't want.. 64

Notes 65
Acknowledgements 69
Author's Bio.. 71

How simple a thing, it seems to me that to know ourselves as we are, we must know our Mothers' names.

—Alice Walker

Forza: A Tale of Two Mafaldas

If anyone needed strength, it was the Princess—
traded in the royal consolidation
game, she was a faceless card swept
into the Scopa deck, falling into the diaspora.
Mafalda of Savoy stood upon a pedestal of crumbling marble

she couldn't hear cracking, until *my God the plane.*
It didn't carry her with honor or even dignity.
What fashionable suit was she wearing
she had to trade for Buchenwald rags? Tyrants
adore their ability to surprise the high born.

You know you've seen this playing out today.
How confounded my mother Mafalda would have been
to know she was the namesake of a Princess bombed
and bled, so busy was she, mourning the loss of her
own strength, a vindictive raven, flying

out of a coal mine in Western Pennsylvania,
worrying the minds of her children, stealing
their language, perching on their achievements.
She might have resented the privileged
Royal Princess if she ever thought of her at all.

Mafalda's Daughter Opens Her Notebook

I have unzipped your mouth
so you can speak to me when
an idea comes
or whisper it on lined paper
brushing my fingers as I pick
up the pen you pushed out
on that first day—

and isn't that the way
a mouth becomes an ear?
and then a hand
and who knows what will be
born next.

Thunder Storms

Can peace be gained until I clasp my wombat?
Dante Gabriel Rossetti

A magnolia unfurls her robe
in the Italian sky above Benevento
a globe of air becomes

temporale. My mother sits
on the basement stairs in Western
Pennsylvania protected from lightning

by a rubber mat;
she prays to Saint Barbara
holding her children too close.

In mother's head-longing
to be American
she left me

on the Appian Way
her teenage gollies and goshes
a dialect I didn't learn.

I wanted the mother language
clasped to my neck like a furry
pet raised in a forever home.

Western Pennsylvania Fig

On
the
wall
above
my stove
is a Pompeii painting under
Plexi
fresco sparrows ready to feast from a basket
of figs,
the basket made from grapevines—the same
vines
my grandmother carried from one land to another.
What world
is in a fig tree contained in soil native to apples?
She did
what they did in Benevento preserving next year's
sweetness, holding the memory of family,
coaxing the growing season for a
second fruiting of umber droops so we
could again sense the missed world—
taste the mineral proof
of heritage.

Queen Elena Has a Baby Girl (Again)

In 1902 a wren was hatched in the royal cradle
so fair was she, fragile as light, strength was
wished for her. A revered old priest baptized
this small bird draped in eyelet. She would grow
into a chick toddling after her mother the Queen
as she ministered to the soldiers during
World War I, rising on their elbows to see
who this child was. This young girl who
back home in her castle learned to play heart-
breaking piano sonatas. Her mother made her
foul tasting tonics that the Princess
secretly poured out into the castle grounds.

Mafaldine or **Little Queens**

This pasta was a fancy
    a ruffled ribbon suitable
        for a delicate Princess.
            In 1902 it was a celebration,
                as if an infant born in Italy
                    was a cosmic occasion
                      requiring all to cook eat
                and digest royalty.
            Mafalda on your kitchen
        shelf meant a place for her
    inside your very being.

Turandot Villanelle

Puccini, was it curse to dedicate
this story of an off-kilter princess
with whom we'd not think to associate

tender Mafalda. Who'd never berate
a lesser man for loving her. Confess,
Puccini, was it curse to dedicate

when you would never learn her awful fate.
You meant to honor Royalty and bless
her sweetness. We always will associate

that aria sung early and too late.
Let no one sleep, no daughter given less,
Puccini, was it curse to dedicate

a paean to her talent with such weight
of music laden with romantic stress
with whom we forever associate

Mafalda. Her numinous dance awaits,
her strong last wishes leaving sweet noblesse.
Puccini, was it curse to dedicate
to the Princess with whom we forever associate

Canaletto Validates my Grandmother

My grandmother said she trained as a stone mason
before leaving Italy at age twenty. On the voyage
from Naples to New York she climbed to the crow's
nest of the steam/sail ship. I learned in Psych class
immigrants inflated their pasts; I learned the limitations
of being female. But, the stone wall Annunziata built
with her five sons still holds back earth in the ghetto
ground. Canaletto at the Met: in the catalog I examine
"In the Stonemason's Yard." There is a red face woman
wet sleeves rolled polishing a marble baptismal font.

Mafalda at Twelve

Mafalda Curzi's memories in her own words at age 70 (1981) at her daughter's request:

I was about 12 year old when my Mom decided that I could help her with sewing chores. So, every July or August she would buy bolts of material on sale suitable for making boy's shirts. Then the sewing machine, old treadle model, would be placed on our front porch with me sitting in front of it, ready for action. Mom would cut the different parts of the shirts and tell me where to sew, to put it together. She would cut the material without a pattern! In no time a shirt would be ready. We made dozens of them for my 5 brothers (while they attended elementary school.) It was a good experience and it was so comfortable on our front porch. The neighbors and friends would keep stopping in for a chat while we worked. This will always remain a beautiful memory.

We worked hard at home with five boys, three girls (two died) I remained to help Mom with all the chores—like washing clothes, no washing machines then. We wrung out those big sheets by hand after washing them in a round tub. We used washboards and our hands. Golly, I was thrilled when the first machines came! Then, we ironed all those men's shirts with irons warmed on first the coal stoves, then gas stoves. Oh, what a job with six males in the house, believe me. I was glad when eventually one of the boys would get married. I was relieved of some washing and ironing as well as my Mom was.

We also had fun at home. Sometimes, in the summer evenings our friends would gather on our porch and we would sing all the popular songs of the day. We sang to the tune of a mandolin played by a friend of my Dad, Nick. Nick was an immigrant also and lived at our house for a while. He had a beautiful voice. The whole street would stop and listen to him sing. Some of the songs of that era were Stardust, Begin the Beguine, Paradise, Moonlight & Roses, and When Your Hair Has Turned to Silver. We had a record player and danced to all the current records.

Mafalda of Savoy at Twelve

You can see in photos how anorexic
she appears. Her legs so thin and straight,
she reins the donkeys as if to master them,
which she probably did waiting for her
prince to come. He's growing up somewhere
in a royal house, she doesn't know which
yet, but she won't rein him, he will win her.

Mafalda Curzi's Autograph Book 1
Graduation from Butler Senior High School May 1927

"There is a girl named Muff
An old maid she desires to be
But this is a regular bluff
For reasons quite plain to see
For although an Italian Maiden
She was born in the "Land of the Free"
With a roguish smile
That puts you hep.
That some young sheik will get her yet
                —Mrs. M.A. Waddell

Miss Reed, Butler High School

Miss Reed flew to school
on a thin white heron
who waited for her
in the mossy garden
behind the library;
she was ghostwriter for the poems
we learned from her. Poems under
pseudonyms like Donne, Milton,
Shakespeare. She kept my mother's
name on a slip of silk paper inside
her maiden bra. She spoke it to me
on the first day of College English, *You're
Mafalda's daughter*, handed it to
me like a pearl on an heirloom necklace.

A Dream of Being a Teacher

Mafalda Curzi's memories in her own words at age 70 (1981) at the request of her daughter:

In High School, I was very active. I loved it. I'd rather go to school than eat, studying every night. The result was I did get good grades. French and Latin came so easily to me. I should have been a French or Spanish teacher. However, the Great Depression prevented me from going on too far into college. There was no work, therefore, no money. Well, I did manage to finish high school with honors. I was second on the list. With this, came more responsibility. I had to write and memorize a speech for Commencement night. It was on the Yosemite National Park, showing slides while I spoke. What an experience! I also served as an editor for our Magnet.

Before graduation, I had applied for the Ritts Scholarship for Slippery Rock College. The ones in charge gave it to one of their acquaintances (not deserving at all.) I was broken-hearted because I knew I was in line for it and had earned it. What's more I needed it so badly! Well, after more than a few tears, I was determined to do something—so I started at Slippery Rock College with a few dollars I earned working in Offutt's Department Store. That money didn't go far but I attended for some credits. I gained a few more credits by attending night classes out of Slippery Rock, also out of the University of Rochester. Reading, Science, History, etc. These Classes were held in our local High School at night.

...Then, Father Marinaro needed a fifth grade teacher. He called me. I was glad to help out. One needed only two years credits at this time. Here, I met Aunt Lena, Dad's sister. She also was teaching at St. Mike's. She invited me to her home and I met my Luigi there.

Mafalda's First Job

Mrs. Barnhart applied her knuckles to the wooden screen door
someone inside said *There's a colored lady
on the porch.* Mafalda went to the door,
she didn't open it. Mrs. Barnhart peered in
told her a call had come in for her
at Paganelli's store down the block.

I imagine Esther Paganelli
behind the counter in her white linen suit,
sign of her rank as a business woman, maybe
the most important woman in Lyndora.

*You better go down there and find out about
that call. No one is coming up here to tell you,
but I'm telling you. I think it's important.*

Like many on the street
the Curzi's didn't have a phone.
Mafalda knew the only person she gave that
number to was the manager at Offut's Department
Store, where she had applied for a job.

Mrs. Barnhart's house was the last one
at the end of Bessemer Avenue. On her way
from the trolley, she had to pass by
all her Italian and Ukrainian neighbors but
she didn't pass by Mafalda. She was kinder
than necessary. I think she probably was one
of the neighbors that Grandpa Joe sold groceries
to on credit during those Depression days.

An Unexpected Dream

Mafalda Curzi's memories in her own words at age 70 (1981) at the request of her daughter:

While working at Offut's Store, I became buyer of the Art Goods, Jewelry and White Goods Departments. My Departments flourished and our Manager was pleased. I also did interpreting for Italian customers. We went from one department to another and the customers would buy up a storm. They appreciated the help. Finally, I got a raise from ten dollars a week to fourteen dollars a week. In those days, that was quite an advancement. But there still was a Depression!

Princess Mafalda of Savoy Considers a Future Husband

She spoke four languages,
learned four musical instruments,
typhoid fever, influenza three times,
all this served to accomplish her.

She was ready for whatever Prince,
would come her way.
He had to be a Royal. There were
only so many options.

There were four sisters to be matched from
the House of Savoy. It was not romantic choice,
but a practicality. She met Prince Philip of Hesse
at a garden party; maybe he did the choosing.

What did she really know about him
except his lineage? Nothing else mattered.
He was an aesthete, a favorite of the Reich.
Did he have hidden sexual proclivities?

In 1925, they married at Racconigi Castle in Roma,
there was smaller celebration for the lesser
villagers. The couple honeymooned on
the Italian Riviera.

Waltzing Mafalda

She complained at times people called her Matilda
because they never heard of Mafalda

She would educate them about the royal origin
of her name: *I was named after an Italian princess*

What she didn't know, not having the Google,
was, before the House of Savoy, the name lived

in countries other than Italy
It really WAS Matilda or Mathilde

with many shortenings like Maud,
(she would have hated that one)

and my personal favorite Tilda
as in Swinton. It was in Italy where

the th was waltzed into f and elevated.

My theory is my grandmother Annunziata
named her for the ancient meaning

"Strength in Battle" because Grandma announced
before everything we did that required

reaching deep, dancing out,
asserting identity

Forza la Battaglia!
with her fist raised

The Wedding of Princess Mafalda of Savoy

She was the daughter
of King Vittorio Emanuele III
she required a royal pairing.

Worn low on her forehead a headdress
fashioned from gold sheaves of wheat.

Her gown was silk gathered at one hip by
a festoon of gems draped to a pointed hem.

Graceful white satin slippers enveloped by
her voluminous lacy train.

Her groom was Philip, Prince of Hesse
grandson of German Emperor Frederick III

grandson of Queen Victoria
lover of poet Siegfried Sassoon

envoy from Hitler to Mussolini,
an aesthete with a decorator's eye.

In the Fuhrer's eye Mafalda was a mote,
"the blackest carrion in the Italian royalty."

And so, Princess Mafalda's wedding became
her funeral, though no one knew this would be.

What is left: a noodle, an opera dedication, a stamp,
a TV mini-series, namesakes scattered in the diaspora.

My Mother's Wedding

Mafalda borrowed her friend Rose's gown
it slipped over her twenty-seven year old
body perfectly. Circling her graceful neck
a Peter Pan collar, puffed shoulders expanded
her aura. Her mother made a veil for her—
held by a lacy headpiece
that framed her heart-shaped face,
now that the depression was ending

they could at least afford that.
I wonder if she wore a corset like the one
she wore every day as we grew up
all those hooks and eyes
the tightening strings.
The wedding took place in the old
St. Michael's church on Spring Street,
Maybe there was a reception up the hill

at the Grippo family Victorian on South.
Mafalda's mother Annunziata,
Luigi's mother Maria Grazia, sister Lena,
made a feast, *zuppe di nozze, panna cotta*.
Father Marinaro was invited to bless
and toast with Grippo wine.
Mafalda's five brothers and Luigi's two
bested each other every way they could.

I wonder, when Mafalda's father Giuseppe
walked her down the aisle did he think of
his other two daughters who died as toddlers,
both named Elvira: typhus,
and a neck-breaking fall off a chair.
Mafalda broke that curse, deserved
her royal name and to be treated
as a precious immigrant princess,

who boarded a train from Butler to Zelienople
with her groom Luigi for a honeymoon
at the famous Victorian hotel there. Mafalda spent the
night in a rocking chair as her virgin bowels
surged her from the bed to the private bath.
And so, Mafalda's marriage became a rocking chair
ticking back and forth but not going far. She told
me years later, He was very nice to me that night.

Mafalda's Mother-in-Law

Maria Grazia practiced the religion
of the countryside,
she may have been *strega* royalty.

She brought her magic from Laurino,
high above Salerno: her tambourine
and her pistol, she was not unlettered.

Her family owned land.
She and Pasquale had goals; they
didn't take shit from anybody.

They knew how to get close to the boss
and then replace him
with themselves.

Maria Grazia shot the Sheriff's deputy
in the knee after she warned him
to stop bothering her.

She could have shot him
anywhere she liked.
Mafalda didn't want her children to hear

these stories as they
were told around the table after dinner,
she would whisper *cafone*, peasants.

Grandma Maria Grazia told me
in my high chair I would grow *bigga
bigga bigga* pinch my cheeks red

her crinkled smile like crepe.
Her coffin was banked with flowers
next to the piano in her living room.

Her red-rimmed
tambourine still hangs
on my studio wall.

The Midwife's Tambourine

When the priest banned
tambourines from the countryside,
you hid yours in the travel trunk under the
Moroccan tapestries and linens of your dowry.
Your Pasquale was thinking America. Wilderness away
from the thumb of Rome and Royalty. In America, you
jangle your tambourine only on Christmas, not ever for
a mother's relief in childbirth. They don't know the uses
of rhythm for their bodies, that power you put away in your
trunk would become a toy until your granddaughter learns
why the drum's rim is painted red, long after her own
children were born. Your Grandmother Gregorio made
that drum, scraped and stretched the goat hide, her
husband carved and bent the wood, cut the jingles
out of tin cans, painted the circle scarlet to
identify its sacred use—it has a history
in blood and water that
will not change.

Pasquale Finds His Wealth

Into the Pennsylvania hills
where Pasquale divined the lay
of the land,
excavated his way into the
black seams,
midwifed the tonnage into
the light,
fed his family for three generations.

Nonna Doula

Pistol in her pocket
she steps out into
the night moon
silent owl shadows
twigs crack under her heels.
She hears her eyelids blink
with each stride
her satchel thumps
against her left thigh
bottles of elixir clink inside.

She counts steps to gauge
her earnings,
the cost of hundreds
of steps in darkness
she never counts in daylight.
She'll soon pull a baby
quiet as a fish
slap it into sound.
When she finishes with this squalling mother
she wants coffee and risen bread

the relief of eating from a neighbor's loaf
the better part of her fee.

From the South American Diaspora, Argentina

Google says comic strip *Mafalda* was named
after a failed appliance brand
but we know better than to believe
that cover story. In that name
was strength, for the battle her creator
Quino was fighting against Pinochet's tyranny.

Imagine Quino drawing a globe to represent
Earth. He draws bandages wrapped around it,
strips of fabric, like a sick mummy.
He situates cartoon child *Mafalda* next to it,
the back of her small hand pressed against the fevered
forehead of this hand-drawn Earth.

Mafalda's grimace worries her face.
It appears she, a child, carries the
burden of sickness herself. He had to stop
drawing *Mafalda's* seeming innocence.
Tyrants recognized cartoon *Mafalda*
as a threat with a following.

Quino said humans have *the capacity to spoil everything—*
If I had continued drawing
they would have shot me once, or four times.
He gagged *Mafalda* in 1974, his family fled to Italy.
When they returned to Argentina She was eventually
resurrected from the tomb of exile.

Princess Mafalda Meets Her In-Laws

They wouldn't attend the wedding
the Landgrave and the Landgravine,
Philip took his *dear little wife*
to Schloss Panker to meet them.

They insisted on the German ritual
escorted by men dressed
in black frock coats
and Digger O'Dell top hats.

On horseback,
through the Schloss in a pouring rain,
a tradition to present the bride who,
saddled with misinterpretations

and foreign language receives this
as a gift of punishment from her groom's parents,
a continuation of her years-long funeral procession,
a sliver of what is to come.

Philip & Mafalda After Dinner with Hitler

Philip
and Mafalda
lived in Italy
in a castle designed
by him, surrounded by
relatives of royal caste. They
had a blast. Tennis, travel, bopping
about in a grand car. He was advancing
up the ranks. Heady stuff to be invited to dinner
with Hitler, and Goebbels. Did Philip notice them nodding
together as they talked about Mafalda? Did he have any idea what
was being said about them, especially her, a fiction of deceit.

Her Luigi

I, Louis, am writing this after my 77th birthday
on November 11, 1981
at the request of my daughter.

I went to Chicago to learn how to be a draftsman
came back and went to night school for machinist
training. I wanted to get married, but I didn't want
to be working for my father in the coal mines.
I started doing tool and die making for him instead.

I designed the coal handling facilities and rebuilt the machinery.
My father died in 1935, my brothers fought each other
for the coal mines. My older brother Tony won. Joe worked for him.
I stayed out of it. My sister Lena cried, she got a job at an
insurance company. I played baseball all those years

and kept to myself 'til, as I said, I wanted to get married.
I got a job as machinist at the Tube Company.
I was employed for two years, during the Depression,
then I got married. When my kids asked me what I did
during the war, I told them I had an essential job.

Enlisted

And what of my mother's brothers
during World War II? They were enlisted
in the chain-gang of industry and war.

The two eldest were in essential jobs,
both in the National Guard:

Fausto rolled steel at Armco across the street
from home in Lyndora. He played trumpet
in a big band before he married Angelina Paganelli.

Armando, was an accountant in the Armco office.
His nickname was Ham. He married Jenny Mustello.

Egidio became a Chief Petty Officer in the Navy,
Pacific Theater. He went to night school on the GI bill.
He became a Superintendent of Schools in New Jersey.
Everyone called him Jigs. He married Mary Mitchell.

Alfonso joined the army. During the war he worked
in an office in California because he could type.
We all had to take typing in high school because of him.
Toots didn't have to fight,
he had a skill! Tootsie was his nickname.
He married Mary Wladika.

Antonio went to Panama with the army. He was the youngest.
He told of giant boa constrictors falling from the trees.
Soldiers shot them to get them off their buddies. *Aim away from him!*
Tony spent months in the VA Hospital in Butler
with a nervous breakdown. He married Janice Fair.

They spoke Italglish. My mother said they murdered the language.
We cousins thought they were being funny, but it's a real thing.
When they came back from the War, they rolled up the rug in Grandma's
living room, cranked the Victrola, and jitter-bugged all over the place.

Little Room Off the Kitchen

From the bottom of my bed in the little room
off the kitchen I watch through the door
that won't stay shut.
Alone, they know what comes next,
speak few words.
In the early morning kitchen, stardust radio on low,
mother and father shuffle on the asphalt tile
dull red grid stained with egg yolk and coffee,
layers of routine, yellowing squares of wax.

                    He puts on clean work socks sitting
                    on the step down to the back door,
                    then his steel-toed boots.
                    He picks up the dented steel lunch box
                    he calls his dinner bucket that never
                    loses that clamshell odor no matter
                    how much mother scours it
                    with baking soda.
                    I hear him leave as I drift back to sleep.
                    She pours another cup of coffee, wipes the table,
                    washes up the dishes.

One morning
reading the Cheerios box
she weeps.
They must have talked about selling.
A new owner would tear up that lusterless tile,
lay hardwood over our history,
but we won't see it because we pack,
move across town to the South Side Victorian
where my father grew up,
where we again spill onto
black and white linoleum
that mother says
shows the dirt.

A Broken Sonnet for Growing Up

My sister overheard her say
she had no hope for any of us
this is what we wrote in dust
when we went out to play.
That dire prophecy meant
I think, since she couldn't
see her future, she wouldn't
tutor us to change, to bend

and so we enacted child's play,
shifting trust for years
on and on we played
until pain brought a clear day:
consciousness and tears.
We knew we couldn't have stayed.

Loss of Land

After Louise Erdrich

a loss of land relates to the souls
who never spoke of love

the strength of ancestors was
their love of me without knowing me

they hoped for me as they planted rows
pinch my cheeks as they visit in dreams

they never speak of their mothers
faces familiar but under-developed

in the photographer's tray
I have to imagine the lineage

describe their hill gardens in mystical terms
say the wet breeze is a mountain wolf's breath

being the last of my family means
I have "conjuring skills"

Autograph Book 2
Graduation from Butler Senior High School 1927

May 29, 1927
"Always bear in mind that under the blanket of deceit the wicked flourish."
—L. L. Paganelli

The Work of Conception

Holding the fragile yolk in a cracked whelk shell
She trudges alongside a speeding train.
The gold breaks, it wants to seep away
She manipulates the spiral to keep the yolk
from draining away into the gravel.
Still, its slight weight draws it down and through,
her palm catches its split viscosity.
When the train passes, she steps across the steel,
releases the egg into the greenest grass.

Happy Times

Here's a photo of Mafalda
with Philip on a *vaporetto* to Capri
She's bundled against the breeze
with her cloche hat and pleated
wool skirt.

Here's another with her
sister Giovanna holding her
in front of the cactus growing
like a bed of thorns there
in the desert.

Here she is in the Villa Mura
alone but for her dog, her arm
like a bent bone draped around
him, protecting, her palm resting
against his shoulder.

In all these photos, there is
a lonely happiness with family.

Princess Mafalda's Children 1940

The Princess wore her motherhood
like a warm surprise, a cashmere
bed jacket in a chilly room. She nursed
her *ultimogenita,* her last born, Elisabetta
wearing three strands of pearls, gazing
at the infant with a sweet curve of her lips.

Mafalda bore three sons for Philip, but it was
la piccola Elisabetta she loved to hold. As toddlers
her boys dressed in sailor collars, had many cousins
to visit and play with. She remembered the photo
of the aunts and uncles with the Balilla in 1940
the children swarming over the car to arrange themselves.

Maurizio, the eldest, on the front bumper,
Enrico the second born, on the roof,
both in short pants, Ottone the third,
nowhere in sight, perhaps napping in the nursery,
Mafalda pregnant with Elisabetta hiding in the back
seat, her smiling face popped out the window

The Princess is Almost

gone that's how ill she is
how starved how thin
she had plenty of energy
but isn't that the way it

goes until they can't
sustain it any longer
and flop down, down.
Was it exhaustion?

A third round of the influenza?
She's depleted from the
childbirth, give her a break,
we'll never learn from what...

She Recovered

> *The goat shall bear on itself all their iniquities to a barren region; and the goat shall be set free in the wilderness.*
>
> *—Leviticus 16:21-22*

If she had gone
to Buchenwald without
the protection
of her royal name
she would have been
sent to the ovens immediately
because she was in no
shape to work.

She was Azazel the goat
going forward into
the wilderness with the
sins of all the others
on her head. She would
take them out to another
battlespace, even though
she was not tethered
to Judaism.

Transported

Her four children remained
in the Vatican, while Mafalda went
to comfort her sister Giovanna in Bulgaria.

While mourning her brother-in-law's death,
Mafalda was accused by the Reich of causing it—
perfidy. He was Bulgarian royalty.

A message from her husband:
Come out to the airport
I'm waiting for you here.

Before she could grab her coat,
two German guards were alongside
not quite shoving her into the car.

She was flown into Berlin with
no breakfast, no warm clothes, no boots,
no husband waiting. Her pleas

for information went unanswered.
There was a new name for her
at the end of her trip.

Later, Philip was picked up,
he was cleared of his crimes
by the de-nazification court.

After two years his sentence was suspended
a third of his property taken. Nazis would
always steal from anyone they could.

It is in their nature.
A small price for Philip's life
that ended in 1980.

Frau van Weber

> *Let me be the thinking heart of these barracks.*
> —Etty Hillesum

They took her silk suit
they took her name, her title—
that rankled them most of all

the pseudonym clung
hung like the woven dress
she was given,

her well-coiffed hair untended
her humiliation intended.
She was there for a year, when

an Allied bomb fell, the trench
alongside the Isolation Barracks
meant to protect the special prisoners

from air raids collapsed around them.
Mafalda, her left side, her left cheek,
burned. She was disinterred alive.

Her last words as she was dug out:
*Don't remember me as a princess,
remember me as your Italian sister.*

She was taken to the brothel building
where Herr Doktor Schiedlausky
cut off her charred left arm

scorched like a bone in a pit.
She never heard the strength
of her name uttered again.

Her life flowed away in the blood
seeping into the Buchenwald
soil from the inept amputation.

*What do I care about Mafalda?
Her intellectual qualities aren't such
that they would charm you—to say
nothing of her looks,* said Hitler

Remembrances from the Princess's Sister and Cousins Roman and Prascia

Giovanna, Mafalda's sister, said:
I was in a profound state of shock.
I am convinced Boris' death
was not criminally provoked.

I gave Mafalda a book
as she left Bulgaria to return to Rome:
Imitations of Christ.
She took that book with her to Buchenwald.

We four sisters had spouses in four different countries,
political argument was tacitly banned
from conversation. My sister, Mafalda was
aware of the drama of the moment living in Italy.

As she left Sofia, holding the letter from her husband,
her last words were *I must think of my children.*
Muti, Mommy was her nickname. Always in good humor,
loved music, played the harp and pianoforte.

Mafalda's cousins Roman and Prascia stated: *Her color was pallid,*
She was always cold, nervous energy, always moving.
She had particularly delicate health.
The day she married, she hid behind columns...

Mafalda had atrophied muscles at the bottom
of her legs, and required a special sole so she
could dance. She adored the fox trot, Charleston,
the shimmy. She ate little, preferring chicken

and boiled potatoes. Official lunches were a
torment for her. She was a maniac about hygiene.
She was intrigued by, first, nature, then family, then society.
She was a simple person soft, generous and optimistic.

We knew how she really was,
the definition from Goebbels
was unfair,
and gross rubbish.

L'ultima Pagina

The last page of the report of Faust Pecorari after the imprisonment and death of Mafalda at Buchenwald.

In quality of doctor I will conclude.
I think that the death ocured [sic] chiefly
because of the Princess' great weakness
caused by the too long operation, because
of the careless [sic] with which the blood vessels
were tied again together, as it should always
be done after an operation. No doctor visited
the princess [sic] during the night of her death
and therefore the secondary hemoragy was not
percieved. I must now add that the dissector
had cut a lock of her hair. He gave a part of it
to Georges Stengher (a french [sic] priest) who left
for Dauchau who kept it in the case where he
kept his glasses. The other part was given to
a Hollander, a friend of Robert Jan. (B1 50)
      PECORARI FAUSTO
      President of the "Me_ catholic
      Association" in Triesta, member of the
      Liberation Comitee of Trieste
      Knight of the Saint Siege

I wish, if this will be possible,
in the future to give a report
to the Pope on the secret religious
activity in this camp, another
report to the royal family on the
Princess herself, and a last one
to the italian [sic] government.

Caption on a Map of Buchenwald

*The oven crematorium where on
the morning of August 29, 1944
the Bohemian priest Father Joseph
Tyl recovered the nude body
of Mafalda as she was about
to be put in the oven.
Padre Tyl was able to deliver
the body to the military cemetery
at Weimar.*

Francobollo, a Postage Stamp 1997

her portrait
a small document
now flying everywhere

The Princess Stars in a Pulp Fiction Mini-Series 2006

The poster is an illustration
drawn retro-style on cheap paper.
Swastikas hang from facades.
The actress "Mafalda" wears
a fedora pulled down to shade her

recognizable face. Her expression
is suspicious, a shifty side-eye full
of guilt. I imagine a track in a minor note
to accompany her trench coat.
The viewer wants to ask:

What was she up to? Was it true?
It's a melodrama,
a romantic trauma.
I can't believe Mafalda was a spy.
She was Muti.

In Herr Doktor Schiedlausky's Words

My memory abandons me.
The trench collapsed on those taking refuge.
The Princess maintained an attitude of composure.
The operation was brief without incident.

The trench collapsed on those taking refuge.
I used minimum anesthetic so her heart could continue.
The operation was without incident, and brief.
The hour she died I believe was five in the morning.

So her heart could continue minimum anesthetic was used.
I don't remember with precision.
I believe she died at five in the morning.
All regulations were followed.

I don't remember precisely.
My memory abandons me.
All regulations were followed.
The Princess maintained an attitude of composure.

Mafalda Curzi's Autograph Book 3
Graduation from Butler Senior High School 1927

Mafalda,
      Be good sweet child,
      let those who will be clever.
      Do noble things, not sit
      and dream them all day long.
      And so make Life, Death, and
      that vast forever, One Grand Sweet Song.

                           Genevieve Leland

Dear Mafalda,
      May God bestow his choicest blessings on our "helper". May He solve the Geometry problems of Life, and after the term is over, help you through your Final Exam and promote you, the next semester to A Blissful Home Room in Heaven.

                           With Loads of Love,
                           Evelyn Conrad

Dear Mafalda,

When your days on earth are ended
And this earth no more you trod
May your name in "Gold" be written
In the autograph of God
                      Your friend,
                      Helen Czep

A Fall on the Stairs

She fell from the stars
when her toddler son
wrested his hand from hers,
tumbled down the stairs.

Luigi picked him up,
slapped her face for
allowing his son,
his first born, to fall.

*But...*she started to explain.
*But nothing! You should've
held onto to him.*
She told me about that shock,

held in her heart, after I divorced,
I supposed in sympathy with
my humiliation, a way
of saying *Me Too.*

How My Father Taught Me My Power

Divinazione dell'acqua:
He wrapped my ten-year-old hands around
two stiff copper wires each bent into an L. I held
the short ends in my fists, long ends pointing out
I walked.

They were like liquid in my hands,
I squeezed as I moved
slowly across the land.
I felt them slipping as I tightened
my grasp.

I held them as firmly as I could,
but they moved anyway.
Suddenly they danced together,
they crossed,
made an X.

He smiled at me. We dug,
the water was there, underground—
You found the water!
Grandpa used to be able to find coal!
Very old magic

I felt connected to a long lineage
of people, some I never knew,
who had expectations.
We didn't have the word for it
in those days. Identity.

Resumption of a Dream

After our childhoods, our adolescent disrespect,
during my younger sister's college years,
my mother quietly resumed her course work.
On nights her classes were offered,
Mafalda worked out at the high school.
Every three credits earned her more muscle.
She got stronger and stronger, until she
gained her teaching certificate.

It was Father Marinaro, that ancient
priest who hired her again.
At her funeral, the Director's daughter
said: *Mrs. Grippo was my fourth grade teacher!*
Her former students spoke up,
one after the other,
revealing this secret life, this *forza*
that could not be thwarted.

Something grew

in my mother's right breast.
She did not give it credence
until an unbearable itch began "down there"
and she had to be examined. She decided
no cutting only radiation, prayer, and a miracle!
It disappeared—
a year later it came back. At ninety
she fell in the breezeway on a patch of ice;

    she moved to Lowrie House.
    Better than a hotel! Someone
    cooked her meals, made her bed, did the wash,
    washed her head, set her perm, called her sweetie.
    Jeopardy every evening after dinner like on
    a cruise ship. She loved the craft room and
    reminisced with two neighbor ladies
    who were also there.

        She fell again, a stroke this time
        she couldn't talk, couldn't swallow water, couldn't
        see much through the degeneration
        of her maculae. I placed a tiny dab of Romolo's
        chocolate on her tongue. She said mmmmm
        and then punched her thigh in anger.
        Because she didn't talk they moved her to a table
        with an Alzheimer's patient who asked

            everyone to find her shoes, but Mafalda was
            still vibrant inside herself.
            I brought a sketchbook for her to check
            a yes or a no to my questions.
            Two years of this and then her breast festered,
            the cancer seized her brilliant brain.
            Hospice in place
            no food water or meds except

a morphine tablet next to her gum and in her
rectum. For ten days I helped to change her diapers
Tell her she can go, says the aide, *maybe she
has some secret sin and is afraid to let go.*
Where do people get these ideas?
I was not going to tell my mother
she could go ahead and die.
This was her last autonomy

Minnesang for Both of Them

No questions in her face
only answers in her eyes
there is no space for lies
Where did our lives go?
This air holds no trace
of a dress made from lace

a lily answers yes
She sees her daughter near
whispering success

Let's sing of her success
only answers in her eyes
her peace is a surprise
Where did our lives go?

Natura Morta

after Giorgio Morandi Still Life 1952

It's been said these paintings are Morandi's family.
But when I look long, it says things are not what they seem,
anything can be re-invented into motherhood,
fragile as painted glass, its potential bursting held firm.

Here are four tall bottles lined up:
two milky mothers dusted
with titanium white
two green glass fathers.
Then a pale celadon sister vase
with swelling hips
insinuated next
to an earthenware brother jug
with jutting handle, sneering lip.
Behind all a tempered black ancestor;
out in front a white china butter bowl—
an infant not yet born.

Once, I thought a window had shattered
and ran from it instead of throwing
myself between my child and flying glass.

After *Time and Space*

We try to imagine the foggy light
the disorientation the stillness
sounds around us
the voices in the room

like family telling stories around
the childhood dinner table
as we doze in the next room
full of ice cream and comfort.

All time is present
like the tail of a comet
we speed up
as we disappear

The sedative cycle of the days...

But today,

today is raw and hot and it stings
the throat. It is called today, but it's really
all our days now.

And behind it is a death trap
waiting for us if we go without
our face covers.

We are we now. We bleed together—
we bleed into streets
we are hit by truncheons

swung by self-appointed goliaths.
Will a ride on the train take us
away to infection

as we flee from the sameness
of the days that threatens
to put us to blessed sleep.

I don't want

to raise the dead, but let me call upon
my mother to answer a question:
> Can you hear me when I call on you, Mafalda?
> Give me a sign. What should I do now, Mama?

Mafalda: You could go to confession. I recall you haven't
> done that in a long time, have you?

Me: Oh, Oy, No I haven't and I don't think I will.

Mafalda: Why do you say Oy? You're not Jewish. Are you turning Jewish?

Me: No, no, I'm not turning Jewish. I just started saying it and now it's a habit.

Mafalda: Okay. Call me again after you've gone to confession. And confess the
> Oy, too.

Let me call on Princess Mafalda:
> What should I do now, Princess?

Princess Mafalda: Listen to the birds of the air, they want not.

Me: That's it? Listen to the birds of the air?

Princess Mafalda: They want not.

Me: Okay. I will listen to them. I hope they say something.

Princess Mafalda: They won't say, they chirp, and whistle, and call. Just be quiet.
> Write down what comes to mind.

Notes:

When my father was recovering from a broken back caused by a pickup truck slamming into his car from behind, I asked both my parents to write about their lives. He was seventy-seven. My father wrote a history of the area where his parents came from in Italy, the mountain town of Laurino above Salerno. He wrote about his family, how they came to America, all the places they lived, where each of them was born, his work life and his relationship with his mother. My mother wrote about her high school days, her good grades, the Scholarship she didn't receive, and her achievements. This is how I knew my parents: my father keeping his culture alive and my mother wanting to bury it.

My mother's name didn't fit the usual Italian pattern of naming after the Grandmother's or a saint. She was a namesake of the Princess Mafalda of Savoy. The name had an ancient meaning: "strength in battle" an apt theme for the Princess and all the Mafaldas in the diaspora. As my mother neared the end of her ninety-two years, I read obituaries, there were three other Mafaldas listed during 2003 in the Star Ledger, Newark, NJ. These women remained in my mind as I began gathering resources.

A variety of serendipitous events gifted me with information. In our mother's cedar chest, my brother found her autograph book from high school along with her report cards. We three children had not known about these most personal treasures. My sister's husband let me know about Quino's death. I found Mafaldene pasta on the shelf at the Basil Bandwagon Grocery store in my hometown after an intermittent search during the pandemic.

I was shocked to discover that Princess Mafalda had died in Buchenwald, a German prison camp. I decided the Princess's story was worth writing about these days when those who would like to live under a dictatorship seek to forget history.

I used the following sources:

Barneschi, Renato: *Frau von Weber: Vita e morte di Mafalda di Savoia a Buchenwald*. Milano: Rusconi Libre, 1982.

Deborah Cadbury. *Princes at War*. UK Bloomsbury Publishing, 2015
Hackett, David A. *The Buchenwald Report*. Boulder CO, Westview Press, 1995.

Katz, Robert. *The Fall of the House of Savoy: The final struggle of an Italian dynasty to preserve its 900-year tradition.* New York: The Macmillan Company, 1971.

Matar, Hisham. *A Month in Siena.* New York: Random House, 2019

Petropoulos, Jonathan. *Royals and the Reich: The Princes von Hessen in Nazi Germany.* New York: Oxford University Press, 2006.

Politi, Daniel. "Quino, Creator of Beloved 'Mafalda' Cartoon, Dies at 88." New York Times, October 5, 2020.

Redmond, Layne. *When the Drummers Were Women: A Spiritual History of Rhythm.* New York: Three Rivers Press, 1997.

Spirituality in the Writings of Etty Hillesum. Etty Hillesum Conference at Ghent University, November 2008.

More specifically:

Turandot Villanelle
In 1924, Puccini dedicated his last opera "Turandot" to Princess Mafalda whom he considered a gifted musician and a sweet and gentle spirit, very unlike Turandot who was known for her cruelty and cunning. Puccini died before he could finish this opera; Franco Alfino finished it in 1926.

Autograph Book 1, 2, 3
In lieu of a yearbook, the girls kept autograph books for writing memories and verses to their classmates who were graduating from Butler High School.

Canaletto Validates my Grandmother
My Mother's mother Annunziata directed her five sons to build a stonewall along the front of the house on Bessemer Avenue in Lyndora, PA. Lyndora was an immigrant ghetto. My grandmother and I stood on this wall many mornings waiting for bread and donuts from the National Bakery truck.

Mafalda at Twelve Mafalda's Memories Written in 1981...
She was seventy when I asked her to write anything she could remember about her life.

I asked my father to do the same.

The Wedding of Princess Mafalda
Adolf Hitler and his Minister of Propaganda, Joseph Goebbels saw the Princess as a threat to the German war effort with Hitler calling her the "blackest carrion in the Italian royal house." Goebbels, for his part, called her "the worst b**** in the entire Italian royal house."

From the South American Diaspora
Joaquin Salvador Lavado Quino was born in July 1932 and died on September 30, 2020 at his home in Argentina.

Epigraph: Etty Hillesum was a Jewish Philosopher who developed her ideas of peace in the face of the holocaust. She died in Auschwitz in 1943. Her diaries were published in 1981. Poet and editor at *Ritual Well*, Hila Ratzabi led a zoom workshop on Hillesum in 2020.

Minnesang for Both of Them
A minnesang is an archaic German poetry form based on singing and dancing

Acknowledgements

My gratitude to the editors and publishers of the following works:

"Thunder Storms" *Mom Egg Review* 18, 2020

"Western Pennsylvania Fig" *Philadelphia Poets*, Vol. 19, 2013 in a different version.

"Pasquale Finds His Wealth" Message in the Coal, Artist's Book, Experimental Print Institute, Lafayette College, 2001

"Canaletto Validates my Grandmother" Honorable Mention in *Passager, 2018, Poetry Contest.*

"The Midwife's Tambourine" Artist's Book, Lucia Press, 2021

"Nonna Doula" *Ovunque Siamo,* 2018

"After *Time and Space*" Video by Jim O'Donnell, YouTube, April 2020

"Miss Reed, Butler High School" Ovunque Siamo 2021 with a different title

"How My Father Taught Me My Power" Ovunque Siamo 2021

"Natura Morta" Ovunque Siamo 2021

MaryAnn L. Miller is the author of *Cures for Hysteria* (Finishing Line Press 2018) and *Locus Mentis* (PS Books 2012), also forthcoming from CW Books, a chapbook titled *Time is a Snake's Tongue* (2023). She has been thrice nominated for a Pushcart Prize. Her poetry, book reviews or essays have appeared in *Mom Egg Review, Wild River Review, Presence Journal, Ovanque Siamo, Stillwater Review, Wordgathering, Kaleidoscope, Passager, Journal of NJ Poets, The International Review of African America Art,* and the anthologies *Illness as a Form of Existence, The Pandemic of Violence,* and *Welcome to the Resistance.* She enjoys reading with the Italian Writers of Boston, New York, and Philadelphia. The granddaughter of Italian immigrants, she grew up in Western Pennsylvania immersed in the diaspora.

Also, a visual artist, Miller was the resident book artist at the Experimental Printmaking Institute, Lafayette College, Easton PA for seventeen years. Her artist books are in the collections of the National Museum of Women in the Arts, Stanford University, Bieneke Library at Yale and many others. Her work is represented by www.ravenfinearteditions.com

She has had Hyperkalemic Periodic Paralysis since she was three years old. It has slowed her down but hasn't stopped her.

www.ingramcontent.com/pod-product-compliance
Lightning Source LLC
Chambersburg PA
CBHW031126160426
43192CB00008B/1123